Grieving at Christmastime

Grieving at Christmastime

written by
Dwight Daniels

illustrated by
R.W. Alley

ONE
CARING
PLACE

Abbey Press

Text © 2005 by Dwight Daniels
Illustrations © 2005 by St. Meinrad Archabbey
Published by One Caring Place
Abbey Press
St. Meinrad, Indiana 47577

Library of Congress Catalog Number
2005926596

ISBN 0-87029-394-x

Printed in the United States of America

Foreword

Christmas comes every year, whether we're ready or not. Joyous though the season may be, Christmas also brings its own special set of challenges and stresses. And when we are grieving the death of a loved one, the season can be especially difficult for us.

This book is intended to help readers understand and cope with the particular challenges a grieving person faces at Christmas, and to offer consolation, hope, and creative ideas for approaching the season in a new way.

The central message here is that it's important to acknowledge, respect, and respond to our grief, even while everyone around us may be rejoicing. The book offers a variety of options to observe Christmas and its many rich traditions in a way that recognizes and commemorates both the season and our grief.

At a time of loss, hope is the greatest gift we can give ourselves or a loved one. Indeed, hope is at the very center of the Christmas message. If this book can help in some small measure to restore hope to a grieving heart, it will have served its purpose.

1.

Christmas is coming.
The signs of rejoicing are
everywhere. People smiling,
people laughing—but not
you. In the midst of joy,
you feel sad. Your heart is
heavy. You are grieving.

2.

Your loved one has died.
Perhaps this is your first
Christmas since the death.
Even if more time has passed,
the grief and sadness can
return at this time of year
with a special force.

3.

Shoppers rush by, their arms filled with gifts. You walk alone, feeling empty. City sidewalks twinkle with color and light. But a light has gone out in your life.

4.

Carolers sing out, "Joy to the world!" But you don't feel like singing this Christmas. There seems to be little to be joyful about in your world.

5.

Holiday cards arrive with messages of good cheer. But they don't cheer you up—not this year. They only seem to remind you of what you have lost.

6.

Fortunately, you don't have to face your grief alone. You can turn to loved ones for companionship and comfort.

7.

Your friends and family understand that you are hurting. They are ready to help in any way they can.

8.

If loved ones are close at hand, you can spend a quiet evening visiting them. Even from a distance, you can feel connected through a phone call, letter, or email. Staying close to those who care helps at this difficult time.

9.

There will be times, however,
when you simply need to
be alone. It's okay to
decline a social invitation.
Your emotional needs
are extra important
this Christmas.

10.

Seek a balance between time alone and time with others. Moments of solitude are helpful, but isolation isn't. Reach out to a friend when you just need to talk.

11.

If decorating a tree or hanging lights is too much for you, find a simpler way to mark the season. Maybe a candle and wreath is enough this year. Don't force yourself to do more than you can.

12.

When you're feeling low, a simple diversion can be good for the spirit. Watch a movie or curl up with a good book if it suits you.

13.

A pet can bring comfort and companionship at a time of loss. Maybe this is the year to give yourself a warm, cuddly Christmas present!

14.

Attending a children's Christmas show at a local school might bring a smile, and that's not a bad thing.

15.

If you feel up to it, offer to help out with the show in a simple way. Raise and lower the curtain between acts, or hand out programs at the door.

16.

Volunteering is a good way to connect with others. You don't have to do much—a little can go a long way toward making you feel better. Perhaps a local soup kitchen could use help chopping vegetables.

17.

Serving those less fortunate at the holidays helps us recall our blessings, even at a time of loss. And our loss gives us extra compassion for others who are hurting.

18.

Some days, however, putting one foot in front of the other is all you can do. But it's enough. Go for a long walk when you're feeling down.

19.

Physical movement helps as you work through your pain. Maybe this is the Christmas to join a local health club.

20.

Take up a new sport, or dust off an old one. Go slow, respect your limits, but don't be afraid to sweat a little bit—it can help with the healing. So can engrossing yourself in an enjoyable hobby, if that's more your style.

21.

A change of scenery can be helpful when familiar surroundings bring painful reminders. Consider spending this Christmas with a friend or relative in another town.

22.

It's okay to take a little holiday
from the holidays this year, if
that's what you need. Maybe
a few days at a lake or on the
shore is the best way for you
to let Christmas gently sail
by this year.

23.

If a friend can accompany
you when you travel, all
the better. It's nice to have
someone around, whether
or not you feel like talking.

24.

You can also "go on vacation" right at home. Spending a quiet holiday in front of the fire, or nestled in your favorite easy chair, is just fine, and a nice way to escape the stress of the season.

25.

Maybe you can write a letter or
paint a picture that expresses
your loss. You don't have to
mail the letter or hang the
painting. They are for you.
The point is simply to get
the feelings out.

26.

Some quiet time is good for the soul. Maybe this year the season's spiritual meaning will speak to you in a special way. Light a candle and let the glow fill you with warmth and hope.

27.

Seek ways to commemorate the deeper "reason for the season." Your faith tradition can be a source of comfort and meaning at this time of loss.

28.

Christmas worship services
are filled with warmth and
color that can soothe a
hurting heart. Ask a friend
to accompany you to a service.

29.

Maybe you can join the church choir this holiday season. Being part of a group gives strength at a time of loss.

30.

But when everyone around you is rejoicing, grief can come on unexpectedly. Be gentle with yourself if you find yourself overwhelmed in a crowd. Step outside for some fresh air.

31.

Remember that it's okay to change or even skip some traditions this year. If you'd rather wait until later to exchange gifts, loved ones will understand.

32.

Other people are grieving this Christmas, too. Look for a bereavement support group in your area. Sharing the pain with others who understand can bring comfort and peace.

33.

In the process, you may find new friends who also wish to observe Christmas in a different way this year. Together you can make plans to help each other through the season.

34.

Find a way to memorialize your loss this Christmas. It could be as simple as putting a loved one's name on a stocking and hanging it on the mantle. Or perhaps you'll want to plant an evergreen in the garden.

35.

A gift in your loved one's
name to a children's charity
will help needy families
express their love to their
children at the holidays,
and it will help you
feel better, too.

36.

Remember that it's perfectly OK to feel happiness and joy, too, at Christmas—right in the midst of your grief. Your loved one would want you to feel merry.

37.

The sky will clear. And in the night, you will see a star shining in the dark. Your loss has meaning. There is hope. Love never dies.

38.

One day, peace and happiness will return to your troubled heart. Just as surely as day follows night, a new dawn awaits you, beyond the grief and the pain.

Dwight Daniels is an author and editor of spirituality publications. He can be contacted by writing the publisher of One Caring Place / Abbey Press Publications. He would like to dedicate this book to his brother Ted, who is grieving the loss of a loved one this Christmas.

Illustrator for the Abbey Press Elf-help Books, **R.W. Alley** also illustrates and writes children's books. He lives in Barrington, Rhode Island, with his wife, daughter, and son.

The Story of the Abbey Press Elves

The engaging figures that populate the Abbey Press "elf-help" line of publications and products first appeared in 1987 on the pages of a small self-help book called *Be-good-to-yourself Therapy*. Shaped by the publishing staff's vision and defined in R.W. Alley's inventive illustrations, they lived out the author's gentle, self-nurturing advice with charm, poignancy, and humor.

Reader response was so enthusiastic that more Elf-help Books were soon under way, a still-growing series that has inspired a line of related gift products.

The especially endearing character featured in the early books—sporting a cap with a mood-changing candle in its peak—has since been joined by a spirited female elf with flowers in her hair.

These two exuberant, sensitive, resourceful, kindhearted, lovable sprites, along with their lively elfin community, reveal what's truly important as they offer messages of joy and wonder, playfulness and co-creation, wholeness and serenity, the miracle of life and the mystery of God's love.

With wisdom and whimsy, these little creatures with long noses demonstrate the elf-help way to a rich and fulfilling life.

Elf-help Books

...adding "a little character" and a lot
of help to self-help reading!